KT-407-873

o freelance

ow to succeed at being your own boss

Go freelance

How to succeed at being your own boss

A & C Black • London

First published in 2008 by
A & C Black Publishers Ltd
38 Soho Square
London W1D 3HB
www.acblack.com

Text copyright © A & C Black Publishers Ltd 2008
Cover image © Martin Shovel **www.creativityworks.net**

A CIP record for this book is available from the British Library.

ISBN 978-0-7136-8855-9

Design by Fiona Pike, Pike Design, Winchester
Typeset by RefineCatch Limited, Bungay, Suffolk
Printed in Spain by Graphycems

This book is produced using paper that is made from wood grown in
managed, sustainable forests. It is natural, renewable and recyclable.
The logging and manufacturing processes conform to the environmental
regulations of the country of origin.

Contents

Are you cut out to be a freelancer?

Answer your question and work out your score, then read the guidance points overleaf for advice on how to get the most of going freelance.

What attracts you most to the idea of going freelance?
- a) The money! Surely there'll be lots?
- b) I like the idea of working from home more.
- c) I've always wanted to be my own boss.

What, if anything, is putting you off?
- a) Finding new work.
- b) I worry about feeling isolated.
- c) Nothing. I think I'd slip into a new working life easily.

The idea of being responsible for your own business is…
- a) Terrifying. I'm not sure I could handle that amount of responsibility!
- b) Good but daunting. That said, I'm sure my confidence would grow over time.
- c) Amazing! I'd love to be in charge of my own destiny in terms of work.

Do you have good organisational skills?
- a) Not at all! But surely my clients will help?

b) I find it easier to be organised about the aspects of my career and personal life that interest me.

c) Yes. I'm always very on the ball.

How confident are you about making decisions?

a) Hopeless. To be honest, I try to get other people to have the final say.

b) So-so. I feel better taking decisions that aren't too important.

c) Very. Not everyone agrees with them, though.

Can you work well under pressure?

a) No, I get stressed out easily when I'm under too much pressure.

b) I have always been good at working to deadlines but like to keep myself clear of unnecessary pressure.

c) Yes, pressure motivates me to work effectively.

Do you find it easy to stick to your to-do list at work?

a) It depends on how enthusiastic I am about what needs to be done!

b) I'm easily distracted from mundane tasks.

c) Normally, yes. I understand that some tasks will be a bit of a drag, but it all balances out.

How do you feel about being responsible for your own accounts?

a) It's been the aspect of freelancing that's been putting me off the most. I just don't know where to start.

b) It's not really my bag, but that's what accountants are for!

c) I reckon I'm organised enough to manage my own accounts successfully.

a = 1, b = 2, c = 3 Now add up your scores.

- **8–14:** You seem a little reluctant to face up to what going freelance really means in terms of responsibility: it'll be up to you to manage your time, make decisions, network, and find new customers to keep your workflow going. Chapters 1 to 3 offer useful information on self-evaluation so that you can really think long and hard about whether it's the right move for you. You also need to be realistic about the money situation: it may take up some time for the work to start coming in, so make sure you have an emergency fund, just in case.

- **15–19:** You are on the right lines, but need to boost your confidence somewhat! You're wise to know that there are some areas you need to brush up on, and managing your time well is the cornerstone to a happy freelance life. Turn to chapter 5 for more help on this. If you're worried about doing your accounts — and many people are — turn to chapter 8.

- **20–24:** You're very confident about your skills, which is great. Once you're ready to move your sights away from the day-to-day work to the future, chapter 7 offers insights about how to make new business contacts that will help you build up work for the months and years ahead. Also, even if you're happy looking after your finances, you may need extra assistance if some customers take their time paying. Turn to chapter 8!

Do you want to be your own boss?

There are many different reasons why you might think about leaving full-time employment and becoming your own boss. You could have had enough of a formal, corporate environment, for example, or want to run your own business.

Whatever your motivation, you'll need to reflect on whether or not you've got the skills to manage yourself effectively, and in this book we'll explain how to do just that.

The advantage of working within an organisation is that it provides you with a career path whilst offering you the structure, systems, and resources that help keep your career moving along. Also, if you're in an organisational environment, you'll get a regular salary along with a range of benefits. If you work for yourself, on the other hand, you'll have to create your own structure and systems and be able to cope with an irregular flow of income. Being your own boss also requires 'big picture' clarity, lots of energy, and a great deal of self-discipline. However, the rewards

are great if you have a desire to take charge of your working life and a healthy ambition to go with it.

Step one: Think about your motivation

You may be contemplating entering the world of the freelancer for a number of different reasons, some of which may have more to do with 'escape' than 'aspiration'! Although your initial motivation may be to get away from a difficult situation, check that this isn't the *only* motivator for you to become self-employed—otherwise you might find yourself trying to move forwards whilst looking backwards.

If, however, your current (probably not ideal) circumstances are merely encouraging you to do something you've always wanted to do, perhaps it's time for you to take action. Ask yourself the following questions to check whether you want to make a change for the right reasons:

- Have you dreamed of being your own boss for a long time?
- Do you think you'll be able to make better use of your talent and experience as an independent person?
- Is there an opportunity you wish to take advantage of?
- Do you have a role model or mentor who inspires and encourages you to go it alone?
- Do you have a great business idea?

- Have you invented a product or a process that you think will form the basis of a business?
- Do you come from a family of entrepreneurs?

Whether the trigger to be your own boss is positive or negative, try to have a positive vision of the future. If you can manage this, you'll easily find the amount of energy and commitment that you'll need to succeed.

TOP TIP

Many people dream of leaving the rat race and living an idyllic life in a sunny climate. However, the majority fall foul of their dream so if your ambition is to work for yourself abroad, think very carefully first. Will you be able to adapt to a foreign culture and lifestyle? Are you up to speed on the legal aspects of owning and running a business abroad? You need to be totally committed, with everything planned properly. Being on holiday is very different to living and working abroad, so get advice from others who've done it before jumping in with both feet.

Step two: Have you got the qualities a freelancer needs?

How well do you know yourself? Although this may seem like an obvious question, it does no harm to review your values, beliefs, and talents—and think about what drives you—to ensure that you'll be able to rally sufficient personal resources to sustain yourself in self-employment. Try to imagine what it'll be like to be your own boss and what qualities you'll need to be successful. The following questions will help you to focus on whether freelancing is the right choice for you:

1 Are you happy to be the sole decision-maker?
Often, people who manage themselves find it quite hard to have to take responsibility for every decision that has to be made—large or small. In larger, organisational settings, there are usually precedents to follow or you can bounce ideas off colleagues. If you're working on your own, you won't have this luxury.

2 Do you like to be alone? If you're going to be self-employed, you'll need to be happy to be alone and autonomous, and enjoy having choice and control. While this is generally true for most freelancers, some do return to a more traditional office or workplace arrangement because they miss the buzz of being around others and the support of collaborating with others who are working towards the same goals.

3 Do you have the organisational skills? Being your own boss demands a great deal of organisation. You'll need to plan your time to include your marketing and networking activities so that work will continue to flow. In addition, you'll need to make sure that your books are kept up to date and that you can put your hands on the paperwork related to your finances. You'll need to deal with invoicing and general office administration efficiently, as well as investing in and maintaining the technology that helps you to communicate with the outside world. All this is before you even begin your work!

4 **Are you persistent and disciplined enough?** The more tedious aspects of being freelance aren't exactly motivating — but they're still important. Sometimes, you'll have to be strict with yourself to keep going when you'd rather stop and relax for a while. In truth, you're rarely off duty when you run your own business and if you don't attend to the administrative or work-related issues as they arise, they'll just pile up until they become urgent.

5 **Do you complete projects and assignments on time?** Remember that you'll have no one else to blame or cover for you if things get on top of you and deadlines slip. You're only ever as good as your last piece of work, so you'll have to maintain the goodwill of your clients by troubleshooting and delivering on promises. If you're going to miss a deadline, you'll need to manage your client's expectations so that there's no damaging fallout.

6 **Will you be able to market yourself by building and managing your network?** It's very common for people who work on their own to dislike networking.

Not surprisingly, this is especially the case for shy people, who can find it gruelling to contact people and build their network. Yet networking is a vitally important activity. If you're to remain on the radar screen of clients who wouldn't otherwise see you, you need to be proactive and arrange meetings so that they can build a relationship with you face to face.

If you can reply 'yes' to the questions above, then there's a good chance that you'll make a success out of going freelance—or at least, there's no harm in making the leap forwards.

Step three: Be clear about what you want to achieve

Most people need a structure and incentives to work: without them, it's all too easy to let things slip. When you're freelance, you'll need to provide these things for yourself. Make sure you know what you want to achieve and what you'll gain by doing so. In terms of your approach, the most important quality is self-discipline and a commitment to what you choose to do. You need to be able to keep yourself focused and productive even if things aren't going particularly well from time to time (as they do for everyone).

TOP TIP

Some people want to work for themselves but still retain links and be under the 'umbrella' of a larger organisation. If this rings true for you, you might want to consider buying a franchise. However, make sure you do your research properly and find something that will hold your interest for the duration of the franchise agreement. It's easy to buy a franchise, but they come with a tangle of legalities which are hard to back out of. Talk to some of the existing franchisees and visit the website www.startinbusiness.co.uk/franchise.htm for advice on buying a franchise.

Step four: Think through your financial and contingency plans

There are likely to be ebbs and flows in the amount of work you're commissioned to do, particularly at the outset when you may not have the experience and stability that will guarantee your continued success. There are key areas you need to consider before you take the plunge, such as:

- **Do you have a good business proposition?** This isn't so vital if you're leaving full-time employment and are going to carry on doing the same type of work in your new freelance life, but it is essential if you're aiming to set up your own business and need to raise funds from a third party. If this is the case, you'll need a business plan (see p. 11 for a helpful link). Remember to include contingencies that will help you get through the lean times as well as the good.

■ **Do you have a good grasp of possible risks?** You need to be fully aware of what might go wrong and have thought about the ways in which you might be able to get yourself out of a tricky situation. For example, it may be a good idea to take out professional indemnity insurance, which protects those who provide professional advice or services.

■ **Do you have a good support structure?** Families are often the casualties of those who are committed to making their own businesses successful. It's very easy to fall into the trap of neglecting your private life when you first go freelance. Making sure you have a support network, whether it's your family or a professional network, can make all the difference.

■ **Do you have health insurance and a pension?** When you work for yourself, you don't have the safety net that employers provide if you get ill or when you retire. So you need to think about these right at the outset of your self-employment. Don't be an ostrich!

■ **Have you made provision for your taxation and accounting obligations?** Many people find it challenging to take responsibility for their own books, particularly in the context of today's complex fiscal laws. It's a relief, often, to be able to hand these over to a specialist and it doesn't always come at a high cost. However, there are many accounting packages and taxation advice is available freely if you choose to take on this aspect of your business.

TOP TIP

You don't have to form a company when you become your own boss, but when you start working for yourself you must inform HM Revenue and Customs (HMRC) within three months. Go to www.hmrc.gov.uk/selfemployed for information on how to register.

Becoming your own boss requires robust motivation and brings with it high levels of responsibility, commitment, and energy. It's easy to focus on the more burdensome aspects of working for yourself, but there are also pleasures. Every time you win a piece of work or are awarded a new contract, you'll know you've done it for yourself. Your earning capacity is as great as you wish it to be and you can choose when you spend time away from your work and when you go on holiday. Although it's hard work, the rewards are in direct proportion to your skills and abilities. There's a lot to recommend it!

Common mistakes

✗ You think you'll get rich quick
Some people see running their own business as a quick way of making money and, because of this, they

get embroiled in opportunities that promise an early return and lots of riches. However, it's important that you aren't seduced by the apparent glitter of a business idea that you know little about. Make sure that your venture operates in an area about which you are knowledgeable and passionate.

✗ **You don't reserve funds to pay your tax bills**
When cash flow is poor, you may be tempted to steal from your reserves to get you through the lean time. However, this puts you in danger of being left short when your tax bill is due. Make sure that you calculate and cater for your tax liabilities as you go along and if you think you're getting into trouble, consult with an expert who can advise you on the best way forward. HMRC, Chambers of Commerce (see p. 12), the major banks and independent small business advisors are useful resources in these circumstances—so do make use of them.

✗ **You go freelance or decide to start a business without making plans**
Many people rush into a business and make it up as they go along. But more often than not, this leads to disaster. Make sure you think through the business opportunity from all angles and write a detailed business plan, which will force you to highlight any areas of vulnerability and consider them before you commit yourself. It doesn't mean you won't take a leap into the freelance world, but it *will* mean that you're prepared and can cater for most predictable eventualities. There

are many resources on the Internet that offer guidance on how to draw up a business plan.

STEPS TO SUCCESS

✔ If you're considering going freelance, make sure you have a clear vision of your objectives.

✔ Think carefully about whether you have the characteristics and determination to work effectively outside a traditional corporate culture—it isn't for everyone, yet suits some people tremendously.

✔ If relevant, write a business plan. Always consider all the financial implications—how will you get through bad times, do you need insurance, and so on—before you take the route to self-employment.

✔ Remember that a dream and enthusiasm are not enough to ensure success. If you have dependants, it may be worth taking on some freelance work or setting up your own business alongside your usual job for a while. Although this may delay the beginning of your self-employment, it contains the risk long enough for you to work out whether you really can cut the mustard at being your own boss.

Useful links

British Chambers of Commerce:

www.chamberonline.co.uk

Her Majesty's Revenue and Customs (HMRC):

www.hmrc.gov.uk

Writing a business plan:

www.planware.org/businessplan.htm#5

How to write a business plan:

www.bplans.com/dp

MSN money, '6 steps to being your own boss':

http://articles.moneycentral.msn.com/
RetirementandWills/EscapeTheRatRace/
6StepstoBeingYourOwnBoss.aspx

Smallbusiness.co.uk:

www.smallbusiness.co.uk

Reinventing yourself

As discussed in Chapter 1, when some people go freelance, they still operate in the same 'world' as they did previously. This is particularly common following redundancies, or company restructuring. For other people, though, a complete change of scene is very appealing: if your career's been in a rut, or if you've been through a turbulent time at home or at work, reinventing yourself may seem to be the key to a fresh start. That new beginning might result in you going freelance, but before you take the plunge, there are lots of things to consider.

As a word, 'reinvention' implies a process of deconstruction followed by reconstruction, and a resultant new thing or—as in this case—a new person who exhibits different talents and who pursues different opportunities. The intended 'payback' for reinvention is gaining something that you currently feel is missing in your life. This could be anything from a successful career, to a better financial situation, to a happier work–life balance, or a completely new lifestyle.

Reinventing yourself as a *reaction* to something or to a set of circumstances tends to result

in a purely cosmetic change as it doesn't get the root of *why* you want your life to be different. In order to reinvent yourself successfully and for the right reasons, you need to do it consciously and deliberately rather than as a knee-jerk reaction. This doesn't mean for a moment that spontaneity and creativity have no role in a life change—indeed, they're valuable forces in this process—but building in reality-checks as you go along will do you no harm at all.

Step one: Take stock

Many of us arrive at decision points in our careers unexpectedly. For most people these days, the planned career path is a myth. It's unusual to find someone who decided what they wanted to do with their careers when they were at school and then followed the recommended route to get there. When people talk about their jobs, it's much more common to hear how amazed they are at what they've ended up doing—listen out for how many times you hear the phrase 'I just seemed to fall into it!'. It's not surprising, then, that many of us eventually realise that we're not doing what rewards us professionally, emotionally, culturally, or spiritually.

The pressures of modern life drive us towards making choices that bring an illusion of security, status, and success. We find a 'good job' and are sucked into the promotional slip stream while being paid an increasingly large salary for taking on additional responsibilities. At the same time, we accumulate benefits such as private health care and company pension schemes which make us reluctant to change our lives radically. Once we realise we're unhappy, we try to rationalise our way out of it, convincing ourselves that we've invested too much in our organisation and our careers so far to risk starting again at the beginning. So we struggle on, perhaps resentfully, fantasising about how it could have been. If only . . .

Sometimes, we're 'fortunate' enough to be assisted in overcoming our resistance to change. We're made redundant, we suffer ill health, our family circumstances change, a significant relationship comes to an end, and so on. This external trigger often results in personal reinvention—and is often perceived to be a blessing in the long run.

The challenge for most people is to arrive at the decision to make adjustments in their lives *before* such a dramatic catalyst intervenes. Being able to sense the imbalance in your life, the drawbacks of your current job, and the gulf between who you are and who you've become is key to making meaningful personal changes. In this way, you can be conscious of what you're doing, why you're doing it, and the likely pay-offs or penalties for doing so.

Below is a process to help you through the reinvention process:

1 Do a personal audit

It's time to appraise your life from a personal and professional perspective. You could think of it as a 'force-field analysis', where you write your name in the centre of a clean sheet of paper and itemise your life's pressures and disappointments on the left and the pleasures and delights on the right. Write down everything you think is relevant, including the interests and aspirations that you had early in your career and all the things that have given you happiness since then.

From this activity alone, you may be able to see where unacceptable pressures lie but if you can't, highlight the 'break points' on both sides of the analysis in a highlighter pen so that you can easily identify the issues that really need to be addressed. The intention here is to find a way of swinging the balance of your life towards the pleasurable side of the diagram by drawing out the elements of your life that characterise you and your preferred role.

2 Explore your values and beliefs

If something's preventing you from tapping into your natural talents and living your life in line with them, write it down at the bottom of the sheet of paper. These are the barriers that you have to overcome in order to achieve satisfactory reinvention. They usually manifest as fears, for example: 'I'll lose my income/pension/benefits', 'I have a dependent family and can't risk letting them down', 'I've hefty financial commitments and won't be able to meet these if I go freelance', or 'I can't afford to go back and start something from the beginning at this stage of my career'.

TOP TIP
All the above are fears that you hold without question. So question them. Are they *really* true? Do they *really* matter? If you live your life according to these beliefs, how will you feel at the end of your working life, freelance or not? Is this acceptable to you?

---

3 Think about your dream scenario

Think about what you'd do if you were free from practical or financial limitations and write everything down at the top of your sheet of paper. This is a freeing exercise that may put you in touch with what it is you'd prefer to be doing. Don't censor your ideas or cast them aside on the basis that you don't have enough money or security to achieve them. Put barriers to one side and remember that with a little imagination and inventiveness, there are ways around the perceived obstacles of money and security.

Step two: Plan carefully

If you like the work that you're doing already, you're part of the way there. In your case, you don't need to 'reinvent' yourself, but 'retarget' your career. Your objective is to plan carefully for a freelance life.

---

1 First of all, think about your current skills and what you'd like to pursue.

2 If you feel there are gaps in your knowledge, ask yourself how you can fill them. Would you benefit from more training? Should you try to gain additional experience on-site before you leave the company you're working for? For example, perhaps you could arrange to shadow a colleague who has the experience you're hoping to gain.

3 Once you've done your research and are clear about what you want to do, think about how you can make the personal changes you've identified.

Do make sure you've got the experience you need before you take the plunge and go it alone.

TOP TIP

Once you've decided to become a freelancer and will be working for yourself from now on, you'll still need an up-to-date CV. For example, you may well find that a new client is open to the prospect of working with you, but wants to see your CV before they commit. Or they may have to sell your services to a third party. So update your CV regularly and remember that you can always rewrite it as often as necessary so that it's more targeted and relevant to your current situation.

Step three: Start making changes

Now you've done the thinking, you can start making changes, small or radical. Working through the process above will have allowed you to see your life laid out in front of you and should help you pinpoint the areas that need the most immediate attention. If you've a strong feeling about the need to change something but aren't clear why, don't try to reason your way out it; follow your instincts and see what happens.

If you curb your impulses by rationalising them, you'll end up behaving in the same way time and time again. To others and indeed to yourself on some levels, your actions may not stand to reason but see what happens anyway—many people have benefited from taking risks at certain points in their life. Taking action first and reflecting later has probably been the pattern of your career to date so try something new, see if it works, then adopt or discard your initiative as appropriate.

Step four: *Live* the changes

It's no good deciding to make changes but then not doing anything about it. Even if the changes seem alien to you to begin with, practise them until they feel normal. Act as if you're the best artist in your field, the greatest writer, the most successful entrepreneur—whatever it is you want to achieve. It's mind over matter; once you start behaving like the person you want to be, people will start treating you as if you *are* that person.

TOP TIP

You can't change your life without changing your behaviour patterns, and this may feel strange to begin with. If you find this too hard, try starting with symbolic changes like your clothing, your hairstyle, or your car. You could even throw away the television! By doing this, you'll create new reactions in others, or you'll find that you're introduced to new people who will help draw you further into your desired—freelance—self.

As you work through Steps one to four above, you'll see that reinvention isn't really what's going on here. The *effect* is reinvention; the *fact* is that you're bringing to the surface a latent part of your character that seeks full and happy expression. Make the decision to live the way you want to—fully and without apology. What's the worst that can happen?

Common mistakes

 You rush it

Some people decide to make radical changes in their lives and jump into a reinvention of themselves noisily and clumsily. This only leads to disappointment. Although enthusiasm is vital for any attempts at personal change, it needs to be balanced with considered decisions and a deep understanding of yourself. Without these, you'll make changes that don't last and end up feeling disillusioned and apathetic. Work through the process above and ask a trusted friend to help you if you feel you're getting lost along the way—someone else's perceptions and feedback can be very helpful in keeping you on track.

✗ You feel pressurised by others

There are many pressures driving people towards feeling inadequate if they don't do something 'momentous' with their lives. There's no 'rule' for what you should be, however, so don't get pushed into reinventing yourself for the wrong reasons. Always make sure that it's *your* choice that is driving your desire for change and not external pressure or some 'ideal' that you've adopted. Being happy with who you are should be your objective, not change for change's sake.

✗ You pretend to be something you're not

Reinventing yourself isn't just a marketing exercise, although it may help you to market yourself successfully in your chosen professional area. People are quick to pick up on others who they think are just 'putting on' a new personality or way of acting, so be who you really are, for the right reasons.

STEPS TO SUCCESS

✔ Assess your values and beliefs and identify anything that prevents you from fulfilling these.

✔ Know the ideal situation you would like to live in and decide what you will need to change to get you there. You need to be focused on your objectives before you go freelance.

✔ Don't over-rationalise—follow your instincts and take action.

✔ Don't rush the process—if you take your time and think carefully about what you'd like to achieve, you're much less likely to run out of steam if things don't change immediately.

✔ Don't be pushed into radical changes by other people. What works for them may not work for you.

✔ Change only for you and to be the person you really are.

Useful links

Fast Company:
www.fastcompany.com/online/29/reinvent.html

Fiona Harrold:

www.fionaharrold.com/course_information/
reinvent.html

iVillage.co.uk:

www.ivillage.co.uk

PsychotherapyHELP:

www.nvo.com/psych_help/reinventyourself1

Do you have the right personal skills to go freelance?

Setting up your own business can be very rewarding, but there are pressures involved. It's not enough just to have a good, viable idea: you also need to have the right skills and temperament to make the opportunity succeed. Starting your own business is also a risky thing to do, so you need to be aware of what problems to look out for as early as possible. This will help you decide whether you're willing and able to take those risks, and will also help you to apply strategies that will reduce them.

It's time now to do some important self-analysis. Be honest and objective, and discuss your proposed career change with friends, colleagues, and relatives. They may know your strengths and weaknesses better than you do! Think about how you've dealt with past challenges as an indication of how you might respond to difficult new situations. This chapter will help you work out whether you have the right skills to go freelance.

Step one: Think about your personality

While the technical aspects of your business will require specific qualifications, skills, or experience, there are broader demands that are as important. These could include the ability to negotiate with suppliers, be sociable with existing customers or convincing with prospective ones, think clearly under pressure, take criticism on the chin, portray confidence, and use your time effectively.

There's no single type of self-employed person, but experience has shown that there are some characteristics which successful self-employed people often have in common. They tend to be logical, perceptive, organised, and responsible. They're usually extrovert and confident, and able to communicate and get their point across. They're also often sociable, with the ability to lead. Self-employed people are generally single-minded, but able to take advice. They're flexible and adaptable, quick to take opportunities, and ready to take risks. They tend to be tough-skinned, and able to handle failure. They're usually creative and imaginative, always coming up with new ideas for the business, and also hard working, committed, and determined. Finally, they're often individualists, who aren't afraid to stand out from the crowd.

Does any or all of the above sound like you? Check how many characteristics can be applied to your own personality. The more you can tick off, the more likely you are to be successful when you start your freelance life.

TOP TIP

Surveys reveal that many successful businesses
have been started by people in their 30s with
only a little management experience. People
over the age of 50 (sometimes called 'third-age
entrepreneurs') are also responsible for many
business start-ups—often they think about
a change of direction only after taking
early retirement.

At the other end of the spectrum, young people
have fewer domestic commitments, plenty of
energy, new ideas, and the potential to develop
and adapt to the challenges of self-employment.
So it doesn't matter how old you are when you
go freelance. All you need is commitment, an
objective, a thought-through plan of action, and
the right personal attributes!

Step two: Consider what skills you'll need

You'll almost certainly need technical skills in your freelance
life. If you've qualifications relevant to your business activity,
this will obviously be helpful. Customers, and anyone
lending your business money, will be much more
comfortable if you can show that you've had relevant
training. Additionally, certain businesses require exceptional
ability, such as design, artistic, or linguistic skills.

Commercial knowledge is a huge advantage. When you're freelance, you'll need to understand the principles of business and management, including marketing, strategic planning, accounts, personnel and people management (you need to get on with your clients even if you don't employ staff), and so on. Ideally, you should aim to get some basic training in business administration before you start. If this isn't possible (and few people have the time or money initially), then read as much as you can to fill any gaps in your knowledge. Leadership skills are important, too. If you expect the business to grow, you'll ultimately employ people, and the ability to lead your team well and to manage people will be critical.

All businesses require an element of selling, and you'll need to develop skills in this area if you don't already have them. Initially, you'll need to persuade people to support you, and it's crucial that you're able to win over potential customers. It's possible to learn basic selling techniques, but being outgoing and articulate are a good start.

Your organisational skills will also be essential to your success. To generate sufficient income, small businesses must be well run and efficient. It's vital that you can keep on top of things, plan ahead, and manage your time— and be extremely careful not to over-promise, particularly in the early days, when you're looking for work. You also need to have the discipline to set and meet deadlines. Try to think laterally about how many of these skills you have, and don't be put off too easily. Becoming self-employed is challenging, yes, but think about the skills you already use in everyday life and how you could apply them to a different context. For example, if you're a woman with a family, or one who has juggled full- or part-time work with family life, think about how you've developed your time-management skills, probably without even noticing it!

Step three: Assess your abilities and resources

Going freelance does involve taking some risks, so you should get to grips with them as early as possible. This will help you decide whether you're willing and able to deal with them and will also help you to apply strategies that may reduce the risks. You need to ask yourself several questions:

- Do you have the necessary financial resources, and can you afford to risk them? For example, you might take a secured loan based on the value of your home; what are your plans if your business fails and you're forced to sell the roof over your head?

- Do you have the experience and technical skills to perform the core functions of your business without the support networks of a corporate employer?

- Are you familiar enough with the market to be able to assess its needs and adapt to its changes?

■ Do you have the tenacity and discipline to see through
  hard times when cash will be short and demands will
  be heavy (from customers, bankers, and, crucially, your
  family)?

While you might not be able to answer all these questions
completely, it really is important that you're honest and
objective about yourself. If you've identified gaps in your
knowledge, step four below will explain how you can fill
them!

Step four: Consider professional training and support

Assessing your skills is a useful process as it'll help you
identify areas in which you need training. These in turn
will contribute towards your chances of being successful
when you're self-employed. There are many sources of
training available to small businesses, and several
courses are run by local colleges and universities. The
Internet is a great source of business information, and you
could start your search at **www.yell.co.uk** for 'Training
Services'. Also bear in mind Trade Associations and Sector
Skills Councils—they may run industry-specific courses.

Advice on, and assistance with, training is available from
local Learning and Skills Councils (LSCs) in England,
Education and Learning Wales (ELWa), Local Enterprise
Companies (LECs) in Scotland (contact Highlands and

Islands Enterprise, address below, if you live in Northern Scotland) and the Department for Employment and Learning (DEL) in Northern Ireland. Many of these organisations will also be able to provide details of any loans and financial assistance available to help with training for small businesses.

Business Links (Business Gateways in Scotland, Business Eye in Wales, Invest Northern Ireland), Chambers of Commerce and Enterprise Agencies will often run business courses and provide information on training providers.

Step five: Be prepared for the pressures

The pressures of being self-employed are inescapable. You may have to work long hours, and there will be times when things get on top of you. You may well get into debt in order to finance the enterprise. You'll need to maintain your faith in your self and your business, often in the face of other people's doubts.

There may be times when you feel lonely and isolated. If you employ people, you'll need to be positive and show leadership even when you least feel like it. Sometimes, you'll need to be tough and prepared to make difficult demands of your suppliers. You'll need to be polite and helpful, even when an awkward customer is being difficult.

Many individuals who successfully start their own business have the backing of their nearest and dearest. You'll be under pressure and your family must be prepared for the impact this can have on family life—especially if you have to work long and antisocial hours. Also, you must be sure that your family can accommodate the risks that self-employment can bring, especially in terms of lower income in the initial stages, and maybe even the implications of the business failing. Take time to talk to everyone who might be affected by your choice to be your own boss.

Common mistakes

✗ You assume that being your own boss will be easy

At some point, most people come across a boss who makes their lives difficult, but don't assume that working for yourself will be all plain sailing. Yes, there are many benefits, but you'll have to get used to the idea that the buck stops with you. Make sure you're ready take on that responsibility.

✗ You go freelance for the wrong reasons

Whatever else you do, don't go freelance for the money alone. Weigh up the pros and cons of your plan and the impact that being self-employed will have on all areas of your life. It will take a lot of effort, but you *can* do it if you really want to.

STEPS TO SUCCESS

✔ Think seriously about whether you've got what it takes to be your own boss before you do anything rash. Have you got the right sort of personality? Do you have enough self-discipline and tenacity? Ask those closest to you for their opinion.

✔ Consider your skills—do you need to acquire any new ones before you go freelance? Will you be able to handle the financial side of the business? Are there any courses you could take to improve in areas where you fall short?

✔ Check your support networks. Have you got financial agreements or funding in place—just in case you have to survive a downturn? Will your partner, family, and friends support you, especially when you're starting out? Talk things through with those you trust and you're much more likely to be successful.

Useful links

Business Eye (Wales):
www.businesseye.org.uk
Business Gateway (Scotland):
www.bgateway.com
Business Link (England):
www.businesslink.gov.uk

Chambers of Commerce:
www.chamberonline.co.uk
Highlands and Islands Enterprise:
www.hie.co.uk
Invest Northern Ireland:
www.investni.com
Learndirect:
www.learndirect.co.uk
Learning and Skills Council:
www.lsc.gov.uk
Sector Skills Development Agency:
www.ssda.org.uk

Managing your time effectively

If you work for an employer organisation, the systems, and overall structure that you need to do your job, will already be in place. They may not be perfect, but at least they're there! When you go freelance, on the other hand, *how* you work, *when* you work, and *for how long* is completely up to you. No one else is going to create a framework for your working day, or set up the relevant systems that underpin your projects.

Deciding how to work is a bigger challenge than it may sound, particularly if you've spent most of your career so far working in a traditional office environment. And unfortunately, you won't be able to escape dull or repetitive work completely—you'll need to do all the admin tasks that'll keep your business afloat, so it's essential that you budget in some time to deal with them.

That said, there's plenty you can do to make your freelance life just as effective as when you were working for a company. You need to analyse your working patterns and prioritise all aspects of your work, so that you get the job done but still

have some time for yourself. This chapter will give you useful tips on how to do this. The underlying factor is that you'll need to bring some discipline to your day-to-day working life!

Step one: Reflect on how you work best

We all have a tendency to put most effort into jobs that we really enjoy, hoping that the less attractive tasks will somehow magically fit in around them. To get a real handle on how you're managing your time, create a 'task diary' and make a note of the tasks you're doing and the amount of time you spend on them. Look carefully at the 'shape' of your day and look objectively at what you're doing. In what ways could you be working more effectively? Can you see what you're neglecting and what you're spending too much time on for little return? Are you focusing on the most profitable parts of your business? Once you've spotted some trends, make a commitment to adjust your working pattern for the better.

Step two: Plan your day

One easy but powerful way to do take control of time management is to create a to-do list that covers all your main bases. Some people prefer to do this as they shut up shop for the day, others as soon as they start work in the morning: it doesn't matter when you create your list, as long as you stick to it.

Once you've got a list of what you need to do each day, it'll help you focus on the job in hand and finish what you start. This is especially true if you're prone to being distracted by interruptions. Your to-do list is a key part of good time management, but you need to combine it with some other techniques so that you can manage interruptions better. For example, rather than have your e-mail inbox open constantly, why not set aside specific times of the day to check it? That will mean that you're not tempted to drop everything whenever an important-looking message pops up.

TOP TIP

Don't forget to plan for time away from your desk—everyone needs to take a break every now and again, to recharge their batteries and top up energy levels. In fact, your clients will benefit from it, as the quality of your work will remain high. So make sure you take time out to enjoy your favourite past-times, whatever they are.

Step three: Put some boundaries in place

If you're in a busy patch and have plenty of work coming in, it's very easy to get so bound up with your work that you forget you have a personal life. Mobile phones and easy e-mail access can mean that you're constantly connected to the world of work, and some people find it hard to draw a line at the end of the day. It's important that you keep some sense of perspective, however, and remember that your family and friends are a key part of your life, too. Your health will also suffer, if you don't take regular breaks.

Set up some parameters around your working day and talk to your partner and family, so that they know you're as interested in them as you are in your job. However, if you find that you're disturbed by family members dropping in to pass the time of day, politely but firmly remind them that you're working (even though you're at home!) and that you'll see them later for lunch, a cup of tea, or whatever. If your phone is the major culprit for regular interruptions, don't be afraid to turn it on to voicemail until you've finished whichever planned task you're working on.

TOP TIP

Don't be tempted to put off unappealing work tasks by suddenly finding that you need to mow the lawn, clean behind the fridge, or paint the garden fence. All of these jobs will waste a few hours, for sure, but you'll still have to do your invoicing when you've finished them!

Step four: Be realistic about what you can achieve

Although your business will stand or fall depending on the effort you put in, don't aim for goals that are just unrealistic and which you know, deep down, you won't be able to reach. It would be great to answer all e-mails within three hours of receipt, invoice clients every week, and attend four networking breakfasts a month, but you know your schedule and you know your foibles. It's good to 'stretch' yourself, of course, but don't go to extremes.

Similarly, even though you may think that you can handle every aspect of your freelance business personally, there are some jobs that a professional will always be able to do more easily and more professionally. Employing an accountant to help you tackle your tax and other financial obligations will be a wise investment: rather than plough hours into learning the accounting ropes (and running the risk of not doing it properly), ask a professional to help instead and invest that time more wisely in looking for new work.

TOP TIP

Freelance life often takes on a 'feast or famine' shape, so remember to think beyond your current job, however lucrative it is. What are you going to be working on next? If you're not sure, why not ask your client for a referral? A personal recommendation can be worth its weight in gold. As the project starts to wind down, you'll have more time to start putting out feelers and to amp up your networking.

Common mistakes

✗ You indulge yourself

One of the most appealing aspects of working for yourself is the thought that you can concentrate on what you enjoy most. That's true, but you need to work at balancing all aspects of freelancing life so that the issues that don't interest you as much—but which are still vital, such as invoicing or networking—don't fall by the wayside.

✗ You don't keep your skills up to date

Refreshing your existing skills and gaining new ones is a valuable activity for all freelancers, however busy they may be. Whether you attend a course or seek the support of a trainer or coach, see it as a good use of your time and a great way to keep up to date with industry trends and to meet new contacts.

✗ You don't keep on top of the paperwork

Even if you're absolutely hectic, it's essential that you keep on top of your accounts. The sooner you invoice, the sooner you'll get paid: it's as simple as that. Keep a record any expenditure you incur while you're working on a project, and make sure you keep receipts in a safe place (this doesn't mean the glove compartment of your car!) so that you can retrieve them when you send off your invoice. See chapter 5 for more advice.

✗ You don't try anything new

Many people go freelance because they have great skills in one particular area, and they're keen to exploit their talent as much as possible. That's great, but you may find yourself doing the same type of work for the rest of your working life. Make an efforts to look for new opportunities in related fields so that you can more skills and tap into new networks. You may find that it opens up a whole host of new opportunities.

✗ You have no discipline

It's never appealing to slog away at an uninspiring task, but when you work for yourself, you'll have to do this time and again. There is a positive side, though: if you keep plugging away at all the admin tasks or any other activities you'd prefer not to do, at least they won't build up, so you'll be working effectively. It's a good idea to give yourself a reward when you finish these tasks to help keep up your good intentions!

STEPS TO SUCCESS

✔ Make a to-do list at the beginning of each day—or at the end of the previous day, if you prefer—so that you can focus on what you need to get done and ignore any distractions.

✔ Don't forget to make time for yourself outside your working environment. And don't let work take over your life—otherwise you'll risk becoming a stranger to your friends and family.

✔ Be sensible about how much you can achieve during a normal working week. If you take on too much, the quality of your work is likely to suffer and you'll find yourself unable to meet deadlines.

✔ Don't forget to submit your invoices on time, together with any relevant expenses, and keep on top of your paperwork. If your filing and accounts are in order, you'll find it much easier to stay in control.

Useful links

About.com—How to manage freelance and group consulting practices:

http://consulting.about.com/od/manageyourbusiness/How_to_Manage_Freelance_Group_Consulting_Practices.htm

Andy Budd—Seven habits of highly successful freelance web designer:

www.andybudd.com/archives/2006/10/7_habits_of_a_highly_successful_freelance_web_designer

Freelance UK, Media, Creative, Marketing and PR—Managing to succeed:

www.freelanceuk.com/running_business/managing_to_succeed.shtml

5

Looking after your accounts

Few people are naturally inclined towards
book-keeping, but this can be especially true for
freelancers. Indeed, the attributes of freelancing
have a lot to do with freedom from structures,
systems, and processes. It's about getting to
the point of the work, not focusing on the
surrounding administrative necessities. So, as
a freelancer, you'll probably need to muster
sterling resolve to apply yourself to your
accounts.

However, keeping your accounts in order gives
rise to a sense of virtuousness and satisfaction
and, if you can keep on top of them, they won't
be too onerous in the end.

Step one: Think about some common questions

I'm starting off as a freelancer and I don't know
where to begin to find the information I need. How
do I start?

A good place to begin is at the HM Revenue & Customs (HMRC) website **(www.hmrc.gov.uk/selfemployed)**. You'll find all sorts of information there about becoming self-employed and starting up a business on your own. Also, HMRC run Business Advice Open Days which provide you with an opportunity to get advice and information on running your business successfully. Have a look at **www.businessadviceday.gov.uk** to see if there are any events in your area.

I've worked for an organisation all my professional life, so I've never kept my own books. Where can I learn about how to do this?

If you trawl around the Internet, you'll find many software packages designed for sole traders and small businesses — SAGE is a particularly popular one (**www.sage.co.uk**). Choose a couple and experiment with putting in some fictitious figures—so you can get the hang of each program. If one is more intuitive and easy to use than another, you may want to adopt it. Go for the least complicated version you can find or simply use a proprietary spreadsheet to capture all your financial transactions. It's just a matter of practice.

I'm quite a disorganised person and although I'm looking forward to becoming a freelancer, I dread the book-keeping side. How can I make this easy for myself?

The only way it will become easy for you is if you develop a discipline and a routine. When you come home after an assignment, make a habit of opening your accounting package and recording your expenses. File your receipts and issue an invoice as soon as any work has been completed. Note the amount on the invoice and when it was sent. This way, you can keep track of everything without getting bogged down in bits of paper once a year.

I'm concerned that I'll miss something essential and that I'll get into trouble with HM Revenue & Customs. How can I protect myself?

The only way too protect yourself is to be informed and organised. Visit the HMRC site (address above) and follow the self-employment links. You'll pick up all the essential information this way. If you're confused, used the helplines or consult an accountant to make sure you haven't missed anything.

Step two: Decide on your business structure

Before you even contemplate setting up an accounting system, you need to decide what kind of business you're going to adopt, as this will have a bearing on the accounting system you use. Here are three of the most likely options.

1 Sole trader. This is the most usual business structure for a freelancer, and the most simple. If you're a sole trader, it means that you'll trade under your own name— or a trading name—and that you'll be responsible for your own accounts—regardless of whether you're going to be handling them personally or with the help of a professional accountant. You or your accountant should make sure that your accounts are submitted to HMRC.

2 Partnership. This is the type of business structure that you'd adopt if you were going to work alongside someone else in a formal arrangement. This is a legal entity so you'd need a solicitor to draw up a partnership agreement that could be verified by the government's fiscal bodies. You need to be a little bit cautious when entering this kind of arrangement as both of you are collectively liable for the debts of the partnership—and if one of you defaults, the other will be responsible for honouring the debt.

3 Limited company. A limited company is a viable alternative to the structure of the sole trader and the partnership. With a limited company, your liability is restricted to the share capital of the company. In this way, you're protected from personal bankruptcy should the company fail—notwithstanding any failure on your part to fulfil your duties as a director. If you're starting out with a small concern, forming a limited company may not be recommended for you as there's a heavy administrative load to carry. However, in the long run, if the company is successful and grows, you may find this an efficient solution.

Step three: Set up your business systems

Once you've established the structure of your business, you need to get down to setting up a system to capture all the information you need as easily as possible. You'll need to do the following:

1 **notify various authorities.** Whatever your chosen company structure, you'll need to notify HM Revenue & Customs. As a sole trader, you'll be responsible for calculating and paying your Income Tax as well as your National Insurance payments. In the UK, you'll pay Class 2 National Insurance Contributions (NICs) as well as Class 4 contributions as a percentage of your taxable profits. If you don't earn very much, you may be entitled to the Small Earnings Exception (SEE).

If you're setting up a limited company, you'll need to register this with Companies House and draw up a Memorandum & Articles of Association (agencies will do this for you at little expense). The Memorandum & Articles of Association set out the structure, purpose, and operating parameters of the company in accordance with the Companies Acts 1985 to 1989. When you've registered your company, you'll be sent a certificate of incorporation along with a company number. This should be included on your invoices.

2 set up a bank account. It's really important to set up a separate bank account so that your personal and business monies don't get confused. If you do this, you'll be able to see the ebb and flow of your finances and reconcile your accounts at any time. You can arrange to have a regular salary paid into your personal account if you wish.

3 set up a company credit card. In the spirit of keeping your personal and business finances separate, take out a company credit card so that you don't have to trespass on your personal credit rating when incurring business expenses.

4 establish a good filing system. Good organisation is the key to good accounting practice. Putting things in their proper place and being able to retrieve them again is essential. Keep and file ALL your receipts, just in case HMRC ever want to scrutinise them.

Step four: Use a spreadsheet to keep track of your finances

Using a spreadsheet becomes easy with practice and is an invaluable way to keep an eye on the state of your financial health. Make sure you discipline yourself to enter every single detail of your financial transactions. This is the most important aspect of looking after your own accounts. You'll need to create back-up copies of your spreadsheet regularly; if you don't you'll quickly realise how tedious it can be to re-enter every single invoice! By using a spreadsheet as the cornerstone of your accounting system, you'll be able to:

■ **create invoices.** It's a good idea to create a template that you can use for your invoicing. This should include all your bank details, company number if you have one, contact details, VAT number (if you have one, see below), and so on. See chapter 8 for advice on how to make sure you get paid on time.

■ **keep track of your income and expenses.** Make sure your invoices are sent out promptly and that they contain the details of the work you've done along with any business expenses and mileage you can reclaim. You'll be able to see at a glance whether there are any unpaid invoices that you should chase after the agreed payment period has elapsed. Use your spreadsheet to compare your business activity from month to month and project into the future.

■ don't forget to **record all sales** as they come in along together with, when appropriate, any money from the sale of business assets. Also, record all purchases of business stock. If you take money from the business, make sure you account for this as well as any that is returned to the business from, say, a life-assurance policy. If you take out indemnity insurance to protect you from unforeseen calamities in your work, don't forget to record this as a business expense along with any accounting costs or other professional services.

- **calculate your tax liabilities.** You may have set up a PAYE arrangement with the HM Revenue & Customs, in which case, this will roll on automatically. If you change your level of income, make sure you adjust your PAYE payment. If you have a limited company, you will be liable for corporation tax. Corporation tax isn't paid by sole traders but is paid on Limited Companies' taxable income. Currently, the corporation tax rate stands at 19% for companies with profits of £300,000 or less.

- **calculate your VAT.** If you're turning over more than £64,000 in the UK (for the tax year 2007–08; this figure will change annually), you must register for VAT. Once registered, you'll be sent a registration number which you have to include on all your invoices. You'll need to charge VAT on all fees and expenses you charge your customers. Then you can claim VAT paid out in respect of your own business. You may elect to go for a flat rate which simplifies the process of returning your VAT.

Whatever you do: keep and file ALL paperwork relating to your business and record EVERYTHING on your spreadsheet so that it's up to date at all times.

Common mistakes

✗ You think the rules don't apply to you
Claiming that you didn't know that you had to pay a particular tax or weren't aware of the relevant deadlines is no defence. As a self-employed person,

you're completely responsible for paying the government the various taxes you are liable for and you need to take this seriously. Talk to your local tax office about what's required of you (and when), or seek the advice of an accountant so that you can be ready in plenty of time.

✗ You give up on accounting software too soon
A great deal of time is spent by the uninitiated on getting to grips with the technology. Fazed by apparent complexity, they often resort to a paper equivalent approach which has none of the advantages of a sophisticated accounting package. Spend time getting to know the package you've chosen and perhaps invest in a short course to acquaint yourself with its functionality. When you've learned a particular function, write out a simple crib sheet for yourself so that you can refer to it in the future.

✗ You miss deadlines because of bad time management
You won't be the first if you miss a deadline or a payment due to pressure of work or a lack of resources— but it can be a costly mistake. Be aware of the deadlines and the financial obligations you have to meet and note them in your diary well in advance of the due date. If you think you're going to miss a deadline or a payment, call the appropriate office and discuss it with someone relevant. You may be able to negotiate an extension or a special arrangement—if you do, make sure you take a reference number of the call, your contact's name and so on.

✗ You make your accounts a low priority

Many freelancers think that they'll be able to look after their accounts and calculate and submit their own tax returns. However, if you're not informed or interested in this activity, it's likely to get pushed to the bottom of your list of priorities and become an insurmountable burden. A better option might well be for you to spend your time doing what you do best and appoint a professional accountant to do all your accounting work for you!

STEPS TO SUCCESS

✔ Look at the HMRC website to see what your financial and tax liabilities will be.

✔ Invest in a financial software package that you feel comfortable working with.

✔ Seek professional advice from an accountant or financial adviser if you feel out of your depth.

✔ Don't ignore tax deadlines—and make it a priority to submit your invoices as soon as you've finished a project, supplied your services, or whatever. Don't be afraid to chase overdue invoices.

✔ Keep your business and personal finances separate from each other.

✔ Set up a business account and credit card—this will
  make it much easier to keep an eye on your cash flow
  and will make things more straightforward when you
  have to submit your accounts and tax returns.

Useful links

Companies House:
www.companieshouse.gov.uk
HM Revenue & Customs:
www.hmrc.gov.uk
National Insurance Contributions:
www.hmrc.gov.uk/nic

Looking for work when you go freelance

Going freelance can be an incredibly exhilarating experience, and many people enjoy the freedom and choice that it affords them. On the flipside, it does mean that they're solely responsible for finding work, for balancing their existing workload with the need to find future projects, keep an eye on their finances, and still have a private life!

It can all turn out well, however, as long as you work at building relationships and growing your network of contacts. If you went freelance but aren't a natural networker, going out of your way to meet others for non-social reasons may not be an attractive option. If you don't put yourself out, however, you run the risk of the work drying up one day, so you need build contacts as efficiently and with as little pain as possible. The good news is that there are plenty of ways you can do this, including harnessing the power of the Internet.

In many industries, the traditional hierarchical workplace just doesn't exist any more, which means that the opportunities for freelancers are growing. Yes, it can be a big leap if you've spent the bulk of your career employed by an organisation, but many people find that they thrive in a freelancing environment and eventually have no wish to return to conventional employment in any case! To save headaches and financial crises, however, you need to make sure you have regular work coming in. The steps below highlight ways you can do that.

Step one: Let people know what you can do

Your clients engage you for the range of skills that you have and which they need at that time. Let people know what else you have to offer, however, so that you don't get 'typecast'. You don't have to be pushy, just something such as 'If you're looking for help with marketing/sales/design, do let me know. I used to run the marketing/sales/design department in my previous job, and I'd be happy to talk to you about extending my contract for a few weeks to take this on.'

Another good way of showing how you can contribute further to a client's business is to write a business case that supports your skills and shows how they could be used in a project. If you add some (realistic!) figures to your proposal, you're doing some of the work your clients would have to go away and do themselves, so they'll be grateful for your proactive approach.

Don't be downhearted if this doesn't work when you first try it: no one gets a win every single time, but you can learn from each pitch and improve them as you go forward.

Step two: Tap into your network of contacts

A good deal of freelance work is placed as a result of people's contacts, both close and extended. Take some time to think through the various strands that make up your network: you'd be amazed how many people may be interested in your services, even if only tangentially. Be brave and remind people regularly of who you are, what you do, what news you have, and so on: e-mails, phone calls, and face-to-face meetings are all great ways to do this. As with all networking activity, however, remember that the traffic needs to go both ways. Ask other people how you can help them and they're much more likely to want to help you. And always remember to say thank you for any leads you get.

TOP TIP

If you're reinventing yourself as a freelancer following redundancy, do be careful if your first job is actually with the company that's let you go. Even though you know each other well, you should still ask them to sign a contract with you for the new work you're doing. It's really important to start your new career on a professional footing and also to protect your own interests. Your contact at your former employer may move on,

---

too, if things are in a state of flux, and you'd be wise to have all the details of your project laid out and confirmed in writing. List all relevant aspects that have been agreed (timelines, fees or hourly rates, a description of the work and so on). And remember to include payment terms and any cancellation conditions. Use the final draft of this contract as a template for future contracts.

Step three: Be visible and advertise yourself

Taking the initiative is a key part of freelance success, and as part of your campaign to do that, think about attending events tailored to your industry that will allow you to meet like-minded potential collaborators and clients, too. If you go to a conference, attend debates so you can find out about new thinking, hot topics, and trends. Talk to other delegates and follow up after the event so that you're actively working towards establishing relationships, rather than expecting everyone to come to you. Take business cards with you so that you can give them to new contacts who might offer you future work.

On a similar note, why not offer to contribute to appropriate industry events by giving a presentation or writing an article in the accompanying brochure? Make sure your contact details are listed so that people know how to get in touch with you later. Also, be ready to comment on topical issues relating to your work. While *you* may not feel that you are the 'go to' expert in your field, people will start to perceive you as such.

Step four: Use the Internet

Used carefully, the Internet can be an absolute boon for freelancers. It allows you to find out more about existing and potential clients by visiting their sites, and you can network online too, which is a great option if you're new to networking or unconfident about your social skills (see chapter 7). You can practise online before you try out other networking options. You can also use the Internet to boost your brand, via your own website or perhaps even a blog.

Common mistakes

✗ **You never say 'no'**
When the buck stops with you and you alone in terms of finding work, it can be hard to turn down opportunities. If you agree to absolutely everything, though, you just won't be able to manage. Your standards may slip, clients may be reluctant to give you future projects, and you'll end up losing money in the long term. Be sensible about what you can do well.

✗ **You allow work to take over other areas of your life**
If you're rushing to meet a tight deadline, it's almost inevitable that you'll end up working in the evenings or at the weekends. You'll also need to squeeze in

some time to look after your invoicing, to stay in touch with your accountant, and make new contacts. That's a big to-do list. If it sounds familiar to you, schedule some time in your diary every week during working hours in which you look after these crucial details. Making sure you take regular holidays will also help you rest up and look after your commitments with friends and family, so remember to make time for your social and private life.

✗ You put all your eggs in one basket

Take time regularly to look for new opportunities and customers. Even if you have a fantastic relationship with a large client, there are bound to be quieter times in their work schedule too, and if you rely on them for all your work you'll soon come unstuck. Much of freelance life is characterised by peaks and troughs of intense activity and then fallow periods, so advance planning to keep your schedule more stable is an excellent idea. Don't put off networking or feel that it's a waste of time: being visible and making connections may not reap rewards instantly, but will come in handy eventually. And remember to put out feelers for work as soon as you've completed a big project—even if you feel you deserve a rest, you need to plan what you're going to be working on next.

✗ You don't keep on top of paperwork

Few people enjoy dealing with invoices, contracts, tax returns, and the other admin issues that soak up so much time for the self-employed. Letting this side of your business slide, however, will eventually result in payments being delayed or missed, leaving you to pay for all your outgoings while struggling with no income. If your client has agreed that you can bill them or costs and expenses incurred over and above your hourly or daily rate (international phone calls, say, or travel costs), make sure you keep all receipts and that they are submitted with your invoices. Also, remember that the sooner you invoice, the sooner you'll be paid. Cash-flow traumas are the number one reason behind small business failure, so make sure your business doesn't become another casualty.

STEPS TO SUCCESS

✔ Remind your clients of all your skills on a regular basis and don't be afraid to ask whether you can help on new projects.

✔ Don't sit at home waiting for work to come to you—get out there and meet your potential clients face to face. Make an effort to go to relevant trade fairs and so on. Nothing ventured, nothing gained!

✔ Make use of the Internet to communicate with others and advertise yourself. Although you may not get lucky first time round, the more visible you are, the more likely you are to pick up work when a client is wondering where to place it.

✔ Don't forget to make time for your friends and family. Although you need to work to pay the bills, you still need to make free time for yourself and if you relax properly you're more likely to work more effectively too.

Useful links

How to create a freelancing contract:
http://advertising.about.com/cs/copywriting/ht/ howtocontract.htm
A beginner's guide to freelancing:
www.gyford.com/phil/writing/2006/10/26/a_ beginners_guid.php#h-whentostart

Making the most of social networking

When you go freelance, you'll quickly realise that you can never have too many contacts. You could get your next assignment, project, or business deal through recommendation or word of mouth, or just because someone's heard of you and is aware of your skills. Of course, as explained in chapter 6, you can try to drum up work by recommending yourself to potential employers, but it will do you no harm if you try to widen your network of acquaintances—and this is where social networking can be invaluable.

Social networks have existed for as long as humans have inhabited the planet. There's undeniably 'safety in numbers'! Throughout history, they've enabled us to form stronger tribal and national identities, harvest and hunt food more efficiently, defend our territory, and engage in group activities for fitness, pleasure, and relaxation. These networks also pass memories, learning, and wisdom down the years so that patterns of survival can be repeated without societies having to learn them from scratch each time a new generation is born. These patterns still exist.

Generation 'X', typically defined as those born between the early 1960s and late 1970s, is probably the last generation to have experienced the traditional style of social network. Roughly speaking, this was characterised by relatively stable family units, low mobility, and a kind of constancy that is absent from most of our social networks today.

Generation 'Y' on the other hand, the current '20- and 30-somethings', has been raised in a totally different social atmosphere driven by a high level of technological and material sophistication, instant communication, and global networks that stretch right across the globe. They have quickly become used to both face-to-face social networking and interacting via 'virtual' networks on the Internet.

If you take advantage of social networking, you'll be one step ahead of any competitors who don't. This chapter will point you in the right direction.

Step one: Realise what you stand to gain

You might think that social networking is just an opportunity to get what you want by using other people's knowledge, skills, and talents. But, in fact, it's an important way of making friends, finding contacts, and becoming more involved with both local and wider-scale communities. And having contact with more people than you currently know will help you find work in your life as a freelancer.

Of course, if you constantly use someone for personal gain, they'll soon become tired of serving your purposes and become less willing to help. You may get something from them in the short term—but you're also likely to receive some long-term resentment!. Remember that there may come a time when you *really* need this person to help you, so make sure that the give and take of your relationship is evenly balanced.

You might find social networking a strain if you aren't naturally confident or extrovert. However, if you think of it as a task rather than a pleasure, you may find it less daunting than you expect, particularly if you remember why you're doing it. Network with a clear objective and a strategy—along with a contingency plan in case things don't work out the way you want them to.

Step two: Start networking proactively

You may not have realised how little it takes to set up a social network! Unless you really want to keep your work and personal life separate, the easiest way to start is to join clubs and societies—locally or in cyberspace. Get to know people who might put work your way—once they know what line of business you're in. Attend a few events to get yourself going, and make an effort to exchange information with others. You may decide not to continue with these club meetings in the long term, but the chances are that you'll meet a few new people, who'll then introduce you to *their* social network.

If your network isn't giving you what you want, first ask yourself whether *you* are giving it what *it* wants. Is the effort you're putting in as great as the benefit the network brings you? You may find that you've outgrown your network and that it's time to move on. Sometimes people may be holding you back for one reason or another, or relationships might have started to go sour. Be clear about what you want from your network—and don't be afraid to move on when it's time to do so.

Step three: Understand virtual networking

In the last few years, social networks have metamorphosed from the relatively small confines of family units and close circles of friends to become worldwide virtual communities. There remains a crucial similarity between the two types of network: both enable us to connect with each other in a way that brings more support and opportunities into our lives.

■ **Friend's Reunited** (www.friendsreunited.com) was probably the first important virtual social network on the Internet. Launched in 2000, it grew rapidly and has put many people back in touch with each other by repairing broken social networks in a completely new way. This success inspired the beginning of many more virtual networks where people could find each other and communicate across the globe—as well as across cultures, age groups, and different levels of social, educational, and physical advantage.

- **MySpace** (www.myspace.com) was launched in 2004 and was so successful that it was sold two years later for a staggering $580 million. It uses personal profiles, chat rooms, e-mails, and blogs to enable friends and families to talk online, orchestrate meetings with new people, and or look for those with whom they've lost contact.

- **Second Life** (www.secondlife.com) is a virtual 3-D world built and owned entirely by its residents, registered users who create a virtual persona (known as an 'avatar') of their choice. Avatars take social networking to new heights because instead of reflecting 'real' people, they can be completely invented characters. Since its launch in 2003, Second Life has grown dramatically, and today it's inhabited by over five million avatars.

Step four: Remember the seven principles of social networking

Whether you're networking in person or online, the basic principles remain the same. Think of them as the seven Rs.

1 Reciprocity

This is the 'do as you would be done by' principle. People are much more likely to be willing to befriend and assist you if they feel that their efforts will be rewarded in equal measure. If you want to show your willingness to enter a reciprocal relationship, look for opportunities to respond to someone's interest or need. Try to give unconditionally, and don't pin your hopes on having the favour returned straightaway. If you approach this as a calculated business transaction, you might find yourself being disappointed, but if you give freely, you may be surprised and delighted by what comes back to you.

Don't forget, either, that if you want something, you can ask for it. You don't have to rely on manoeuvring someone into a position where they're compelled to meet your needs. Most people like to be given the opportunity to assist others and are pleased to help out if they can!

2 Respect

Social networking shouldn't be undertaken selfishly or cynically. You may sometimes have to acknowledge that people have a different perspective on life and that your way is not their way. But this doesn't mean that you can't enjoy a mutually beneficial relationship. Try not to be judgmental or dismissive of someone else's values and beliefs, but see things from their point of view. This means not making assumptions, jumping to conclusions or making hasty judgements. Listen attentively to what others have to say and be open to the possibility of changing your mindset.

3 Reliability

When you say you're going to do something for someone, make sure that you honour your promise and deliver. Social networks are voluntary, not compulsory, so it's all too easy to waive a commitment because when there are unlikely to be any negative professional repercussions. However, if you build get a reputation for over-promising and not coming up with the goods, you'll soon find that you won't be taken seriously and others' willingness to help you will diminish.

4 Relationships

Networks are sustained through effective relationships. These can only flourish with good communication, which in practice means staying in regular touch with people and treating them thoughtfully. Show that you have someone's interests at heart by sending them an article they might like, a congratulatory note, or an invitation to an event or dinner. It's very easy to stay in touch more informally nowadays using e-mails and text messages—and don't forget those social networking sites! These are great ways of reminding someone that you're still around, whilst also allowing the person to get back to you in his or her own time.

First impressions are also very important. Remember, it takes only a few seconds for people to make up their minds about you and once they've done so, it's very difficult to shift their perceptions. You may want to think about how you create first impressions and whether these are helping or hindering you. Perhaps you could ask a trusted friend to give you some feedback.

5 Records

If you've got a poor memory, you might find it useful to devise a system that will prompt you when important occasions are coming up for people in your social network. There are many paper and electronic tools available to make sure you keep on top of what's happening when. By being thoughtful and proactive about your communication, you'll be able to demonstrate that you care and that you're willing to put yourself out for the relationship. For example, you might send somebody a message to ask how a particular important event went. Listen out for and take a note of important dates or events when they come up in conversation. Try to be disciplined and record these dates as soon as you hear about them.

6 Results and Rewards

The results of social networking vary from tangible and exciting rewards and opportunities to simply a feeling of inclusion. Be clear about what you want from your networking activities so that you can judge whether or not your efforts are worth it.

7 Review

Social networks are dynamic structures—and they need your attention if you're to get the best from them. Be prepared to raze, renovate, and repair. If you find that one of your contacts is absorbing too much of your time and not giving you what you want, don't continue to pour your energy into the relationship. Sometimes we have to prune our networks in order to keep them manageable. Equally, there'll be times when you need to build your social network. You can do this by attending events, hosting functions, or volunteering your services. Your networks are bound to ebb and flow according to your life stage or circumstances. You may lose some people from your social network and gain others. Sometimes, people reconnect with past relationships years down the line.

The most important thing is to leave people feeling valued. This means being honest about your motivations, and entering relationships sincerely.

Common mistakes

✗ **Your network gets too big**
It may become impossible to maintain all your relationships at once. Rather than run the risk of people feeling ignored or let down, think about how you can manage their expectations. You might disclose that you're going through a particularly intense or busy time and that you won't be around as much as usual for a while. Let people know what's going on for you and then go back to them when time or circumstance allows.

✗ **You can't say 'no'**
If you take on too much for other people, this can leave you feeling overburdened and stressed. You don't *have* to agree to everything people ask of you. Don't over-apologise and be assertive: you don't have

to be rude, but 'I'm sorry I can't help you out with this' should do the trick. If someone presses you, just keep repeating it: they'll soon get the message. Manage your boundaries so that you don't become overwhelmed and exhausted.

✗ You give up too easily

People get disheartened if someone in their network declines a request or is unable to help them achieve something they'd hoped for. Although this may feel a bit like a dead end, ask your contact who they'd recommend you approach next. Hopefully this will put you in touch with somebody new, giving you the opportunity to build even more professional relationships.

✗ You demand too much

Being over-demanding when you have need of a favour can exhaust the good will in your social network. Be vigilant about giving back to anyone who's helped you. If you've developed your relationships well, you'll know just what to do in return, leaving your friend or contact feeling valued and the relationship strengthened. If you're not sure, ask!

STEPS TO SUCCESS

✔ Think about the type of new contacts you need to make and then go out and find them! Join clubs, societies, and groups in person and on the Internet.

✔ Remember social networking is all about give and take. What can you offer others? And what might they do for you? Don't be afraid to ease up contact with anyone who isn't contributing to the relationship.

✔ Show others that you value your contact with them. Sending texts and e-mails are easy yet informal ways to remind people that you exist! Make a note of what's going on in their lives so you can send supportive and interested messages, and always say thank you for any help you're given.

Useful links

Business Networking and Referrals:
www.brenet.co.uk
Chambers of Commerce:
www.chamberonline.co.uk

Making sure you get paid on time

Once you've gone to all the trouble of going it alone, finding new customers, managing your workload wonderfully and so on, the last thing you want is to encounter delays in getting paid. This is (to some extent) part and parcel of freelance life, but you can take steps to minimise the inconvenience along the way, as this chapter shows.

Step one: Understand why you need to issue invoices

Once you've completed an assignment for a customer, get into the habit of doing your invoices as promptly as possible, so that you can keep a positive cash flow and manage your money well. Like a contract, an invoice is a formal record of a transaction between you and a client. It lists the work carried out and the price charged for it and as such is a key financial document for your accounts.

To cut down on queries from customers and also to make sure that you are covered for tax and VAT purposes, clearly show the following information on your invoices:

- an identifying number unique to each invoice

- your name or your business's name, address, and if you're registered for VAT, your VAT number

- date of issue

- your customer's name (or trading name) and address

- a brief description of the work done or goods supplied, along with the price and (if appropriate) the VAT charged

- your payment terms

Make sure you keep a copy of all your invoices so that you can follow up with any slow payers, and also so that you have the information to hand for when you're doing your accounts.

Step two: Chase up payments if they're late

Even if you've always invoiced promptly, there will be times when an invoice just isn't paid on time. The first step to getting your money is to find out what the problem is. For example, it could be because of:

- **a one-off problem.** If a previously good payer suddenly doesn't stump up on time, drop your contact a quick e-mail or ring them to find out what the matter is. It could be something as simple as the invoice not having reached them (in which case you can re-send), someone in the Accounts department having mislaid it or being unexpectedly away, and so on. In most cases, your contact will be able to sort things out quickly once they're aware of the problem, so getting in touch is vital.

- **repeat offenders.** If you pitch for work and are surprised at how easily you win it, it may only be a little while after that you find out why: your clients' last supplier gave up on them after having such a nightmare trying to get paid. This type of client can deploy a whole arsenal of delaying tactics and waste a huge amount of your time as you try to chase them up. One way of minimising the potential risk when you take on a new client is to have a credit check run on them (contact Companies House for help: **www.companieshouse.gov.uk/toolsToHelp/findCompanyInfo.shtml**); this should alert you to businesses going through a tough time. If, however, you decide to give the company a whirl, you may want to charge them higher prices in case you incur extra costs chasing them up, or make them pay on very tight credit terms.

- **a disputed invoice.** Confusion or misunderstandings about the terms of a transaction happen regularly, but can be easily avoided. The best way to do this is to make sure that every step in the sales process (that is, everything from you approaching your customer for work, or them getting in touch with you, and the subsequent discussions about a fee, hourly rate, expenses (if appropriate), time scales and so on) is agreed before you start work. It's good practice to send a quick summary e-mail or letter so that everything is clear for both sides. For example:

Hi Milly

Just a line to confirm that I am free to take on the translation of the widget-building instructions from German into English. I understand that the hourly rate is £25 and that you estimate the work will take 30 hours. I'll let you know if I find it's taking significantly longer than that. Please let me know if any of the above is incorrect.

Looking forward to receiving the text!

Best wishes

Sam Naughton

If you're not clear about this information early on or can't prove that you agreed it, you may have to haggle with the reluctant payer and risk taking a financial hit. If you're sure you have strong case but the client just won't budge, it's time to think about taking a more formal approach to getting your money by going via the small claims court (see below). Keep a record or all your discussions with the late payer, as the court will want to see that you have already tried various ways of resolving the difficulty.

■ your client is in financial difficulty. Unfortunately, this is probably the most common reason for non-payment of an invoice, but may be hidden by your customer behind lots of other reasons. The key thing here is for you to work out whether the problem is a short-term blip or a sign of a bigger and potentially fatal malaise. If the problem is a minor one, it's worth asking your client to pay you instalments over an agreed period of time: it's not ideal, but better than nothing. Again, do make sure that all arrangements are confirmed in writing and then keep checking to make sure that you are receiving the payments as promised.

If, on the other hand, the problem is major, you have to face the fact that you may not get paid at all. Again, going via the courts could be a good option if you make a claim quickly enough. If you have supplied goods rather than services to the customer, you may be able to get them back if you keep a 'retention-of-title' clause in your terms of sale and invoices. For more information, see **www.brethertons.co.uk/ commConFactTitle.htm**.

Step three: Try the legal route

If you've tried every way to think of to get paid but not got anywhere, it's worth taking the issue up with the small claims court if the debt if for less than £5,000.

To get the ball rolling (and to shock the late payer into finally coughing up), inform them in writing that unless you receive your money within seven days, you will be taking legal action. If that bears no fruit, go to your nearest County Court (or Sheriff's Court in Scotland) and state that you want to claim for money owed to you. You will have to pay to make a claim and the fee will depend on the amount in question. For more information, visit **www.hmcourts-service.gov.uk/infoabout/ fees/county.htm**. Alternatively, you can make a claim online, track progress, and receive a judgement online at **www.moneyclaim.gov.uk**.

If you decide not to make your claim over the Internet, the Court will send you a claim form and you'll need to tell them about your business, the debtor's business, the amount in question, and the background to the claim. Be as specific as you can, and back up your argument with all the relevant information you can find. Once you've submitted the claim, the Court will send it to the debtor and then let you know when it was received. The debtor will then have 14 days in which to respond. (If you or the debtor are based in Scotland, you'll have to ask a Sheriff's Officer or Messenger-at-Arms to serve the claim for you.)

If the debtor doesn't respond within the 14 day limit, you can ask the Court to enter a judgement 'in default' and to send the debtor an order to pay you the money you're owed. You can be paid in full straightaway, which is probably the preferred option, but could go for instalments instead: if the late payer has had cash-flow problems, this may be the best route.

Unfortunately, obtaining a judgement is still not a cast-iron guarantee that you will be paid, so if you have further difficulties, ask the Court to enforce the judgement (there is a fee payable for this). A variety of options are open to the Court here, including having goods seized to cover the debt, having a third party who owes money to the debtor to pay you, or even starting bankruptcy proceedings.

Step four: Consider offering an incentive for prompt payment

It isn't appropriate for all freelancers, but in some cases, it may be worth offering an incentive for customers to pay on time as long as (and that's the key point!) it doesn't leave you out of pocket. This route is probably most useful if you supply goods rather than services, and where there is enough of a margin on the price you've given to your client for you to still make some money, even if you give them a bigger discount. For example, let's say your normal terms of credit are 30 days. You could offer a 10% discount to customers if they pay you within 14 days instead. Make clear that this is a special offer, though, so that they don't start to expect it as standard!

Common Mistakes

✗ You put off doing your invoices

This is the quickest way to get into choppy financial waters!
The sooner you invoice a customer or client, the sooner
you'll get paid. It's as simple as that. Few people enjoy
admin, but then again few people enjoy being overdrawn or
not being able to make their mortgage repayments, so get
your act together and set aside some time every week or
month (depending on the type of work you do) to keep
your invoicing in check. Remember that your payment
terms are based on the invoice date, not the date that you
did the work for client.

✗ You're too sympathetic to late payers

Although building good relationships with your clients is an
integral part of making a success of freelance life, you
mustn't put off chasing invoices because you're worried that
you might upset your client. If their business really is in
trouble, you might not get paid at all if you leave it too late. If
you've completed your work to a good standard, you've
fulfilled your side of the bargain, and they need to fulfil theirs.

STEPS TO SUCCESS

✔ Invoice promptly and don't be afraid to chase up payments as soon as they're late, however good your relationship with the supplier.

✔ To cut down on the possibility of queries, check over your invoices before you send them to make sure they have all the relevant details on them.

✔ Rather than sit there and worry, take the initiative and contact customers who are late in paying you. They may not be aware that there is a problem if payments are handled by another department, for example. Make sure you track all your correspondence, though.

✔ If you have no success retrieving your money yourself, it may be worth taking your claim to court. Make sure you have all the necessary information to hand when you start a claim.

✔ Before taking on any large contract with a new client, run a credit check on them.

Useful links

Better Payment Practice Campaign:
www.payontime.co.uk

Credit Services Association (information about Debt Recovery Agencies):
www.csa-uk.com

Her Majesty's Courts Services:
www.hmcourts-service.gov.uk

Where to find more help

Can I Change Your Mind?
Lindsay Camp
London: A & C Black, 2007
256pp, 978-1713678499
Whatever line of work you're in, it's important that your business
communications are as strong and persuasive as possible.
Whether you're writing a pitch, a business proposal, page for your
website, or even a hasty e-mail to a colleague, Can I Change Your
Mind? will help you to argue your case effectively.

Cash Management on a Shoestring
Tony Dalton
London: A & C Black, 2007
208pp, ISBN 978-0713677065
When you work for yourself, keeping an eye on your cash is one
of the biggest challenges you'll face. The good news is that you
can learn how to keep track of where your money is, how to get it
in faster, how to make it work harder for you, and how to cut
costs if necessary.

**Eat That Frog: Get More of the Important Things
Done Today!**
Brian Tracy
London: Hodder & Stoughton, 2004
144pp, ISBN 978-0340835043
Even if you work in an office environment, it's all too easy to put
off unappealing jobs, but when you work for yourself, you don't
have anyone to chivvy you along. This book is a great aid to
making procrastination a thing of the past: the 'frog' refers to jobs
you don't want to do, and the author recommends tackling them
as early as possible in the day so that you can move on to other
tasks.

Give Great Presentations: How to Speak Confidently and Make Your Point

London: A & C Black, 2005
96pp, ISBN 978-0-7136-8257-1

In some industries, potential new customers may ask you to make a presentation about yourself and your work, and this book is a must-read for all nervous public speakers. Full of practical advice and tips, Give Great Presentations will help you prepare well, look confident, speak clearly, and get your message across strongly.

Network with Confidence

Daphne Clifton
London: A & C Black, 2007
96pp, ISBN 978-07136814688

Networking is something that can really improve our career prospects, but many people actively dread it. This book will help you conquer your nerves, ask the right questions, find out about the right events (and work out which ones to avoid), and make sure that the time you invest in networking gives you the best possible return.

Index